THE WORLD
IN THE TIME OF
ALEXANDER THE GREAT

Chelsea House Publishers
Philadelphia

FIONA MACDONALD

First published in hardback edition in 2001
by Chelsea House Publishers, a subsidiary of
Haights Cross Communications. All rights reserved.
Printed and bound in China.

First published in the UK in 1997 by
Belitha Press Limited, London House,
Great Eastern Wharf, Parkgate Road,
London SW11 4NQ, England

Text copyright © Belitha Press Limited 1997
Text by Fiona Macdonald
Map by Robin Carter, Wildlife Art Agency

Editor: Claire Edwards
Art Director: Helen James
Design: Jamie Asher
Picture Researcher: Juliet Duff
Consultant: Sallie Purkiss

First printing
1 3 5 7 9 8 6 4 2

The Chelsea House World Wide Web
address is: http://www.chelseahouse.com

Library of Congress Cataloging-in-Publication Data applied for.

ISBN: 0-7910-6029-2

Picture acknowledgements:

AA & A: front cover centre, title page left, 2, 3, 7 top, 14 bottom, 20 both,
21 both, 22 bottom, 23 top, 24, 25 bottom, 27 bottom, 32 top, 35 bottom,
40 right, 43 top, 44 top, 45 left. AKG, London: 31 bottom. Bridgeman Art
Library: back cover and 39 Zhang Shui Cheng; 4 Architectural Museum,
Istanbul; 16 bottom Louvre, Paris; 23 bottom Museum of Mankind, London;
28 and 43 bottom British Museum, London; 39 top; 44 bottom Bibliotheque
Nationale, Paris. Peter Clayton: 34 left. Comstock Photo Library: 41 top.
C.M. Dixon: front cover right, 5 bottom, 7 bottom left, 13 both, 15 top,
17 left, 18, 19 bottom, 30, 38 left, 42. Werner Forman Archive: 19 top,
25 top, 27 top, 29 top Smithsonian Institution, Washington, 31 top Museo
Gregoriano Profano, Vatican; 33, 34 right Sudan Archaeological Museum,
Khartoum; 35 top Field Museum of Natural History, Chicago; 37 top British
Museum, London; 40 left, 41 bottom Museum für Volkenkunde, Basle,
Switzerland; 45 right. Robert Harding Picture Library: 14 top, 17 right,
26, 27 top, 29 botton right, 38 right, 39 bottom. Michael Holford: title
page centre, 6, 12, 15 bottom, 16 top, 22 top, 32 bottom, 36, 37 bottom.
N.J. Saunders: title page right, 5 top. South American Pictures: 29 bottom left
Tony Morrison.

THE DATES IN THIS BOOK

Today many countries use a calendar that divides
time into two separate eras: B.C. (before Christ)
and A.D. (anno Domino, Latin words that mean
"in the year of our Lord"). It was drawn up
in 1582 by the head of the Roman Catholic
Church. It is based on an earlier calendar
invented by the Roman leader Julius Caesar.

You count forward from the year 0 in the A.D. era,
and backward from the year 0 in the B.C. era.

B.C. ◄——————————— 0 ——————————► A.D.
    2000   1000   1000   2000

All dates in this book are B.C.

CONTENTS

The Story of Alexander the Great	4
The World 500–200 B.C.	8
Time Line	10
Around the World	12
Famous Rulers and Leaders	18
How People Lived	24
Discovery and Invention	30
The Creative World	36
Beliefs and Ideas	42
Glossary	46
Index	48

ABOUT THIS BOOK

This book tells the story of Alexander the Great and looks at what was happening all around the world in his time. To help you find your way through the book, each chapter has been divided into seven sections. Each section describes a different part of the world and is headed by a color bar. As you look through a chapter, the color bars tell you which areas you can read about in the text below. There is a time line, to give you an outline of world events in Alexander the Great's time, and also a map, which shows some of the most important places mentioned in this book.

On page 46 there is a list of some of the peoples you will read about in this book. Some of the more unfamiliar words are also listed in the glossary.

THE STORY OF ALEXANDER

Alexander was born more than two thousand years ago in Macedonia—a warlike, mountainous kingdom on the borders of present-day Greece, Serbia, and Bulgaria. He was a royal prince—clever, strong, and brave—with dreams of turning Macedonia into a mighty nation. Today, more than 2,000 years later, historians call him Alexander the Great.

Alexander lived from 356 B.C. until 323 B.C. But this book covers a longer time span, from about 500 to 200 B.C. During these years the Ancient Greek civilization was very important and influenced many people in Europe, the Middle East, and even parts of Africa and Asia. Alexander admired the Greeks and helped to spread Greek ideas around the world.

◀ This marble sculpture of Alexander shows him as a heroic young man. It was carved at Pergamum, a city that Alexander captured in 334 B.C.

► Alexander may have walked across this black and white floor in the royal palace at Pella, capital city of Macedonia. The pattern was made by using carefully chosen pebbles.

RUTHLESS ROYALS

Macedonian kings and queens were brave and clever, but also ruthless and very violent. Few lived to an old age. Instead, they died in battle, or were murdered by jealous relatives. While Alexander was still a child, he learned how to survive political plots at court. He was guided by his mother, Queen Olympias, who was cunning and wanted more power.

SOLDIER AND SCHOLAR

Alexander's father, King Philip of Macedonia, was a great soldier and a scholar, too. He admired the nearby city-states of Greece and wanted Macedonia to become more like them. He invited the best Greek thinkers to come to his palace in Macedonia to teach Alexander all they knew. Alexander studied science, law, philosophy, and the best way to rule. He also learned how to fight (using the Macedonians' special weapon, a long, sharp pike), how to plan battles, and how to lead an army.

MURDER

Although King Philip respected Greek civilization, he also wanted to capture Greek lands and rule their great cities. In 338 B.C. he invaded and conquered Greece. But while he was away, Queen Olympias most likely plotted to seize power from Philip. At first the plan failed. Philip divorced Olympias and sent Alexander away with her for awhile. But before long Philip was dead. He was stabbed by one of his bodyguards at a grand public feast. Macedonians suspected that Olympias and perhaps Alexander had arranged it, but they dared not complain. So, in 336 B.C., Alexander became king.

◄ Coins often had an image of the country's ruler on them, to spread the ruler's fame. This fine gold coin shows Alexander's father driving a war chariot pulled by two horses.

BOLD PLANS

Persia had been the richest and most powerful nation in the Middle East for more than 200 years. It had the biggest army and had conquered many lands. Persia was also a bitter enemy of the Greeks and Macedonians. As soon as Alexander became king, he made plans to invade the Persian Empire.

Attacking Persia was a bold and dangerous adventure. But if Alexander and his army won, he would become one of the greatest rulers in the world. As conqueror, Alexander believed that he would be more than a king—he would be a god. He visited holy places where oracles claimed they could see into the future. They promised him that greatness lay ahead.

FAMOUS VICTORIES

Alexander was only 22 years old when he set off from Macedonia, hoping to conquer the world. He rode on a magnificent horse called Bucephalus, at the head of a well-trained and well-equipped army. Greek soldiers, fierce fighters from the conquered Greek city-states, joined the army, too. Alexander was a brilliant battle commander, and his army won victories against the Persians at Granicus and Issus. After a third battle, at Gaugamela, the Persian army was crushed, and Darius III, the Persian king, ran away. Now Alexander was ruler of all the Persian lands.

RESTLESS YEARS

For Alexander, conquering Persia was not enough. He spent the rest of his life marching and fighting, winning battle after battle. His journeys were long and exhausting— about 20,000 miles across rough, mountainous territory, mostly on foot. Everywhere Alexander and his army went, they set up new cities. Groups of soldiers settled there, to rule the local peoples.

▲ Alexander spent most of his life on horseback, leading his army into battle or across unknown, enemy lands. As he became more and more powerful, it is said he began to demand that people worship him and his horse Bucephalus as gods.

◄ Alexander's army marched across scorching deserts and over high mountains on their way to India. They passed through this harsh desert landscape, near Persepolis, in 330 B.C.

END OF THE MARCH

In remote Bactria, Alexander married a beautiful princess called Roxana. They had a son, but even then he did not settle down. All the time he wanted to march farther east, to extend his power right to the edge of the world. But Alexander's soldiers were exhausted. When he announced his plans to march across India, they mutinied and refused to go any farther. Reluctantly, Alexander headed for home.

AFTER ALEXANDER

But Alexander never saw Macedonia again. He died on his way back to Europe, in Babylon, in 323 B.C. He may have caught a fever, but many historians think he was poisoned. Roxana and her child were murdered, too, by Alexander's enemies. They did not want Alexander's son to inherit the Macedonian throne.

Alexander was only 33 years old when he died, but he had conquered more and traveled farther than any European ruler before. He and his army also spread Greek politics, language, and learning in far-distant lands. Long after Alexander died, this culture continued to affect the way that many civilizations developed.

▲ The Macedonians fought the Persians at the battle of Issus in 333 B.C. Here Alexander is at the center of the battle, riding his war horse, Bucephalus.

► This map shows how far Alexander traveled, conquering new lands for his empire.

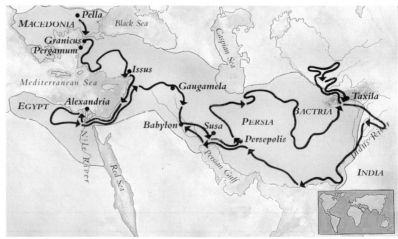

THE WORLD 500–200 B.C.

ABOUT THE MAPS

The maps on this page will help you find your way around the world in Alexander the Great's time. The big map shows some of the places mentioned in the text, including the following:

• **COUNTRIES** that are different from modern ones, such as Persia and Kush.

• *Peoples*, such as the Zapotecs and Scythians.

• *GEOGRAPHICAL FEATURES*, including mountains and rivers.

• *Towns and cities.* To find the position of a town or city, look for the name in the list below and then find the number on the map.

1 Monte Albán	7 Veii	13 Tyre
2 Alexandria	8 Athens	14 Persepolis
3 Carthage	9 Delphi	15 Susa
4 Edfu	10 Pataliputra	16 Sanaa
5 Meroë	11 Taxila	
6 Rome	12 Babylon	

The little map shows the world divided into seven regions. The people who lived in a region were linked by customs, traditions, beliefs, or simply by their environment. There were many differences within each region, but the people living there had more in common with one another than with people elsewhere. Each region is shown in a different color—the same colors are used in the headings throughout the book.

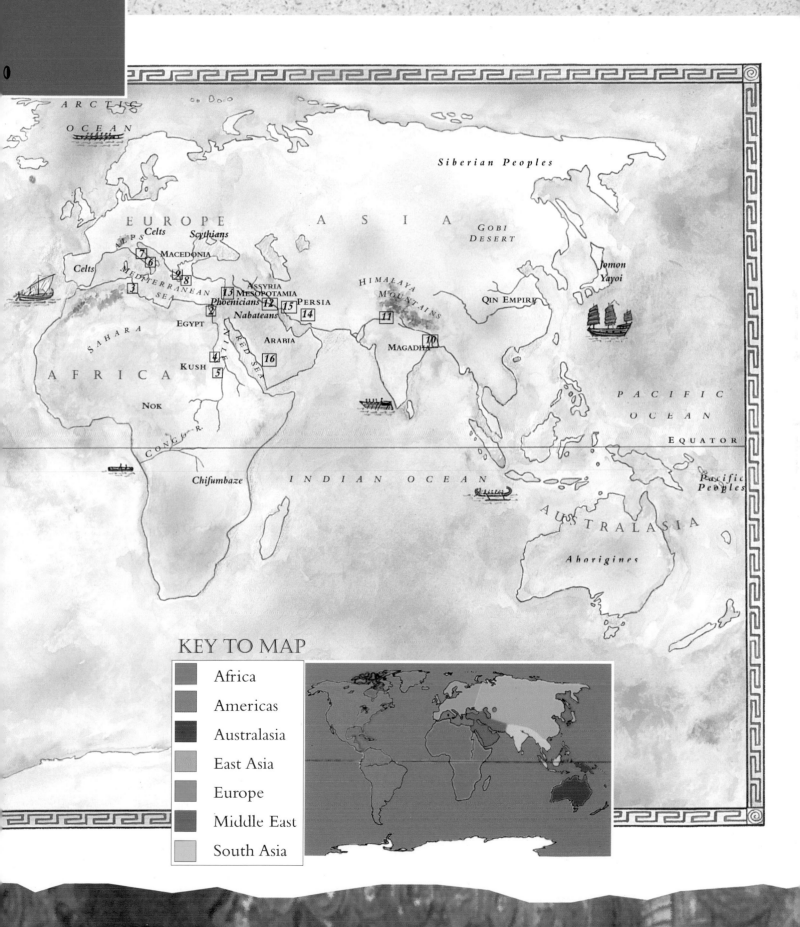

ARCTIC
OCEAN

Siberian Peoples

EUROPE

ASIA

Celts   Scythians

GOBI
DESERT

Jomon
Yayoi

Celts

ALPS   7   MACEDONIA
6

9   8

3   MEDITERRANEAN SEA

13   ASSYRIA
MESOPOTAMIA
Phoenicians   12   15   PERSIA
2   Nabateans   14

EGYPT

SAHARA

AFRICA

KUSH   4   RED SEA   16
5

NOK

CONGO R.

Chifumbaze

HIMALAYA
MOUNTAINS

11

MAGADHA   10

ARABIA

QIN EMPIRE

PACIFIC
OCEAN

EQUATOR

INDIAN OCEAN

Pacific
Peoples

AUSTRALASIA

Aborigines

KEY TO MAP

- Africa
- Americas
- Australasia
- East Asia
- Europe
- Middle East
- South Asia

TIME LINE

500 B.C.   400 B.C.

EUROPE

490 Persians invade Greece but are driven out.

450–350 A great age for the Greek civilization. Many famous writers, artists, scientists, and philosophers live and work in Greece.

400 Celtic tribes from Austria settle in northern Italy.

509 Rome becomes a republic after the last king, Tarquin the Proud, is overthrown.

480–479 Persians invade Greece again, but Greeks defeat them.

c.450 Rise of late Celtic civilization in central Europe.

396 Rome conquers the Etruscans.

461 Pericles becomes ruler of Athens.

447 Greeks begin to build the Parthenon temple in Athens.

390 A Celtic tribe called the Gauls attacks Rome.

MIDDLE EAST

490 King Darius of Persia invades Greece.

c.400 Nabateans found the city of Petra, in present-day Jordan.

522–486 Persia becomes a powerful empire under the rule of Darius I.

480 Darius's son Xerxes invades Greece a second time.

EAST ASIA

479 Religious teacher Confucius dies.

403 The starting point of Ssu Ma Kuang's famous history of China, which goes to A.D. 96

c.500 Chinese begin to use cast iron to make farming tools and weapons.

463–221 Warring States era in China.

c.400s First-known dragon-shaped flags flown by Chinese warriors.

c.500 First Chinese coins made.

c.500 World's first-known hand-knotted carpet buried in a tomb in Siberia.

c.400s First-known canals built in China.

SOUTH ASIA

c.600–321 India divided into 16 important states, called the Mahajanapadas.

c.400 The poem the *Mahabharata* begun.

c.500 First iron-working in Southeast Asia.

c.483 Death of the Buddha.

c.500 Persians introduce new crops, includings peaches and apricots, to central Asia and northern India.

AFRICA

524–404 Persians conquer and rule Egypt.

c.500 Rise of Nok civilization in West Africa.

c.480 A Carthaginian admiral called Hanno explores the west coast of Africa.

c.500 Kingdom of Kush becomes powerful in northeastern Africa.

c.500 First copper-smelting in West Africa.

c.500 Iron-making technology begins to spread through southern Africa.

AMERICAS

c.400–200 End of the once-powerful Olmec civilization, in Mexico.

c.500 Hunters and fishers settle in villages along the coasts of Alaska.

c.500 Zapotecs found the city of Monte Albán in Mexico.

c.500 Adena people of the Ohio River valley begin to build large burial mounds.

c.600–200 Paracas civilization, southern Peru. People weave cotton cloth in colorful designs.

c.400 B.C.–A.D. 250 Early Maya civilization in Mexico and Central America.

AUSTRALASIA

We do not know the names or dates of any people or events in Alexander's time. In Australia, Aboriginal peoples had probably explored most areas by about 500 B.C.

People lived nomadic lives. They hunted and fished in rivers and along the seacoast, and gathered fruits and berries. They carved stones and painted scenes on rocks and bark.

Many islands in the Pacific Ocean had not yet been discovered and settled. For instance, the islands of Hawaii and New Zealand were still uninhabited.

300 B.C.   200 B.C.

359 Philip II becomes King of Macedonia.

356 Alexander the Great born.   **323** Alexander dies in Babylon.

338 Philip II of Macedonia conquers Greece.
338 Rome controls southern Italy.

336 Alexander becomes   **312** Romans begin to build network of
King of Macedonia.   roads linking Rome with conquered lands.

334 Alexander begins his   **312** The Selucid dynasty (family of rulers) now
campaigns against Persia.   rules a smaller, weaker kingdom of Persia.

331 Alexander conquers   **c.300** Bananas (from South Asia)
the Persian Empire.   first grown in the Middle East.

330 King Darius III of Persia   **275** Groups of Celts called the
murdered by his own troops.   Galatians settle in central Turkey.

250 Rome controls all Italy.

218 Hannibal leads an army
across the Alps into Italy.

c.200 A Celtic tribe called the
Parisii founds the city of Paris.

c.300 Yayoi people migrate   **221** Qin Shi Huangdi becomes   **c.200** Nomads from East Asia
to Japan from Korea.   first emperor of China.   introduce horseshoes made of
iron to eastern Europe.

c.300 Farmers begin   **c.214** Building work starts   **c.200** Stirrups used by horse
to grow rice in Japan.   on the Great Wall of China.   riders for the first time in China.

c.277 Chu Yuan, earliest-   **210** Terra-cotta warriors buried
known Chinese poet dies.   in Qin Shi Huangdi's tomb.

c.350 King of Magadha, India, plans   **c.272–231** Asoka rules   **c.200** First kingdoms begin
to conquer a large empire. His plans   **327** Alexander invades India.   Mauryan Empire.   to form in Southeast Asia.
are cut short by Alexander's invasion.

325–324 Alexander's admiral,   **c.250** Asoka makes   **c.200** Expert metalworkers in
Nearchus, sails from India to Persia.   Buddhism the official   Vietnam make Dong Son drums,
religion of his empire.   which show scenes of daily life.

322–321 Chandragupta Maurya
founds Mauryan Empire in India.
Conquers many rich lands.

c.300 Rulers of Kush move their capital   **247** Hannibal born in Carthage.
city to Meroë, in present-day Sudan.

332 Alexander conquers Egypt.   **c.300** Ptolemy founds the   **202** Romans defeat Carthage.
library of Alexandria, Egypt.

c.280 Lighthouse built at Alexandria,
Egypt (one of the Wonders of the World).

264 Carthage begins war against Rome (until 241 B.C.).

c.300 Okvik group of the Inuit   **c.200** Monte Albán now a rich, powerful city.
people becomes powerful in Alaska.

c.200 End of the Chavin civilization,
in the high Andes Mountains of Peru.

c.300 Farmers of the Hopewell
civilization spread along the Ohio   **c.200** Rise of the Nazca civilization
and Mississippi river valleys.   on the coast of southern Peru.

People continue to settle on remote Pacific islands.

Many of the dates shown in this Time Line are approximate.
The letter *c.* stands for the Latin word *circa*, and means "about."

AROUND THE WORLD

Alexander was a warrior. He spent most of his adult life fighting or preparing for battle. He won fame for himself, his soldiers, and even his horse. In other parts of the world, too, successful soldiers won great riches and public praise.

By fighting battles and winning new lands, the armies of Alexander's time helped shape many of the nations that still survive today. These nations fought against one another but also traded across long distances for building materials, precious stones, metals, and food. They shared religions and scientific and artistic ideas.

▲ Greek city-states paid for many beautiful statues and buildings, such as this temple. Rulers believed that people needed to live in pleasant surroundings. Works of art showed visitors how rich the cities were.

ANCIENT GREEKS

EUROPE

The brilliant civilization of Ancient Greece was at its height between 500 and 400 B.C. By Alexander's time it was becoming less powerful, but people were still influenced by Greek customs and ideas. Greece was divided into separate states, which were ruled from cities. Each city-state had its own army and rulers, but the people shared the same language and customs.

For more than 400 years, the Greeks had made the best oil and wine. Greek architects built the most beautiful temples and theaters. Greek rulers encouraged the best scientists, writers, artists, actors, and athletes. Their armies fought bravely against invaders, and Greek ships controlled the seas. They thought all foreigners were barbarians.

▲ Figures of an Etruscan husband and wife, carved on a coffin made around 500 B.C. Tombs show some of the finest Etruscan art. Builders made cities of the dead, with life-size statues of people and sculptured copies of real rooms.

IN ITALY

There were two great civilizations in Italy—the Etruscans in the north and the Romans in the south. The Etruscans were skilled ironworkers and adventurous sailors. They traded with the Greeks and copied many of their customs. After around 450 B.C., Etruscans spent more time fighting the Romans. In 396 B.C. the Roman army captured the biggest Etruscan city, called Veii. By 350 B.C., Rome was the strongest nation in Italy, and Etruscan power was fading away.

FARMERS AND WARRIORS

In northern Europe the Celts lived in small villages and in well-defended hilltop towns. They were farmers, hunters, skilled metalworkers—and fierce warriors, too. Their culture spread from Austria to Spain and Ireland. By Alexander's time the Celts from France had invaded Italy and were also settling farther south, in Turkey and Greece.

PEACEFUL TRADE

MIDDLE EAST

In Alexander's time Phoenician merchants and craft workers lived in busy cities along the coast of the Mediterranean Sea, in present-day Israel and Lebanon. Port towns such as Sidon and Tyre were busy even as far back as 1000 B.C. The Phoenicians were not warlike but grew rich through trade. They sold timber, cloth, precious metals, and carvings. They were also expert sailors and shipbuilders and sailed as far as Cornwall, England, to buy tin.

Farther inland the Nabatean people of northern Arabia also grew rich through trade. They controlled the main routes across the Arabian Desert, used by merchants carrying sweet-smelling incense from Arabia to other lands in the Middle East.

▼ A rich Celtic chieftain once wore this helmet. It is made of bronze and iron and is decorated with gold. Celtic men and women liked to wear bright clothes, jewelry, and fine armor as a sign of wealth and power.

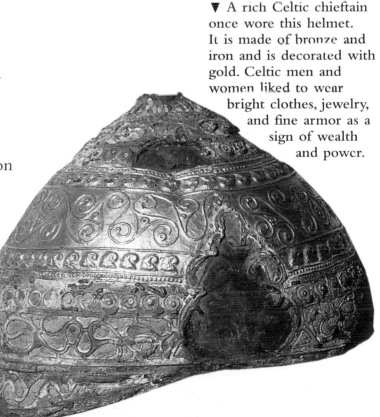

THE PERSIAN EMPIRE

MIDDLE EAST

Until 550 B.C., Persia was ruled from Babylon. Then the Persian king, Cyrus the Great, rebelled and founded the Persian Empire. By the time Alexander became king, some 200 years later, the empire included lands from the mountains of present-day Turkey to the deserts of Iran, from the marshlands of Babylon to the river valleys of northwestern India, and even Egypt.

Persian rulers were proud of their vast empire and called themselves "king of kings." They governed it, with all its many different peoples, very efficiently. They divided their land into areas called satrapies, each ruled by a local governor. They built roads, collected taxes, and ran an efficient postal service. But Persian kings became lazy and satisfied with past success. When Alexander invaded, the Persians were not as able to defend themselves as they had been in the past.

▲ The Emperor of Qin's tomb was guarded by about 6,000 life-sized terra-cotta soldiers. The Qin emperor relied on his army, even in death, to guard his spirit. The statues show how powerful his real army must have looked.

▼ This golden drinking cup is in the shape of a sacred beast called a simurgh. It was made for the kings of Persia as a sign of their royal power. They believed it brought good luck.

CHINA AT WAR

EAST ASIA

In Alexander's time, China was divided into many small kingdoms. They were constantly at war as they tried to conquer one another's land. This period in Chinese history lasted from about 463 to 221 B.C. People called it the Warring States era. Finally, in 221 B.C., a powerful kingdom called Qin conquered all the other states and joined them to form a single empire. The Qin army was led by Prince Cheng, who became known as Qin Shi Huangdi. This means the first Chinese all-powerful emperor. The modern name China comes from "Qin," which is pronounced "chin."

FROZEN SIBERIA

On the mainland of East Asia, in present-day Siberia, wandering peoples survived by hunting wild animals and gathering seeds and berries. Their lifestyle was simple, but Siberian people produced beautiful arts and crafts. We know about them because rich tombs of kings, queens, and magic healers, called shamans, have been found perfectly preserved in the frozen ground.

▲ The peoples who roamed across the cold, grassy plains in Central and East Asia lived as nomads. They were expert horse riders. This wall hanging, found in present-day Siberia, is made of felt. It shows a nomad leader (seated) and one of his warriors (on a horse).

CHANGE IN JAPAN

In another part of East Asia around 300 B.C., the Yayoi people migrated from Korea to Japan. They brought many new inventions with them that helped the craft workers, farmers, and warriors already living there. They brought the pottery wheel, new ways of farming rice, and metalworking skills. Their new ideas mixed with earlier local traditions and began to form a distinctive Japanese civilization.

AN INDIAN CONQUEROR

SOUTH ASIA

When Alexander reached the borders of India in 327 B.C., he found a strong and peaceful civilization. Many people lived in rich cities full of palaces, temples, and lakes. They were well-educated and interested in literature, music, and art. There were also many small kingdoms in South Asia fighting one another for power. Alexander did not stay long in India, but his arrival had a huge effect on a young Indian prince who lived in one of these kingdoms. His name was Chandragupta Maurya. He saw how much a leader like Alexander could achieve if he fought to win power. Chandragupta waited until Alexander died, then drove Alexander's army out of north India and set up his own kingdom there.

▼ The Indian civilization was based on the teachings of the Hindu religion. This illustration, made in A.D. 1761, is from the *Mahabharata,* an adventure poem written between about 400 B.C. and A.D. 300. It teaches that if you are brave, truthful, and loyal you will be a good Hindu. You can see the Hindu god Krishna near the center, wearing a garland of white flowers.

ALEXANDER IN EGYPT

AFRICA

The ancient civilization of Egypt was still rich and powerful in Alexander's time. But Alexander was more interested in owning Egypt's fields and farms, which grew the best crops of wheat and fruit in all the Mediterranean lands. Alexander conquered Egypt in 332 B.C. and built a new city on the coast. He named it Alexandria, after himself, and left it in charge of one of his generals.

THE CITY OF CARTHAGE

There was another great city on the northern coast of Africa called Carthage. At first Carthage was a Phoenician merchant colony, but by Alexander's time it had become an independent city-state. Carthage had grown rich through trade, so it was important that its ships could sail freely across the seas. From 264 B.C., Carthage fought the Romans to keep control of the Mediterranean sea routes between North Africa, Italy, and Spain. After years of war, Carthage was destroyed by Rome in 146 B.C.

▲ Finely modeled heads like this one, made of terra cotta, have been found near Nok. They tell us about people's hairstyles, jewelry, and clothes.

KINGDOMS AND CITY-STATES

In northeastern Africa the rich kingdom of Meroë was a center of gold and ironworking industries. People made farm tools as well as weapons. Between 300 and 200 B.C. the rulers of Meroë built a fine new capital city on the banks of the Nile, with temples, palaces, and tombs made of mudbrick and sandstone.

In West Africa, Nok (in present-day Nigeria) was an important city-state with rich farmlands and skilled craft workers who made iron tools. They also made lifelike terra-cotta figures. These may have been made to be buried in the tombs of important people as a sign of their wealth.

◀ A painted clay mask found in the city of Carthage, one of the main Phoenician trading towns. The people of Carthage did not really look like this. Masks were made to frighten away evil spirits.

▲ This pot, decorated with a pattern of birds, was made by a woman from the Adena people. Pots like these were used to serve food or to decorate rich people's homes.

▶ Carved stone blocks from Monte Albán. They show warriors and Zapotec glyphs (picture writing). The glyphs were carved about 400 B.C. and are some of the earliest text found in the Americas.

RISE AND FALL OF CITY-STATES

In Mexico the Olmecs, who had ruled over a great civilization for almost a thousand years, were beginning to lose power in Alexander's time. Their civilization finally collapsed around 200 B.C., and another group, the Maya, began to take its place.

Also in Mexico the city-state of Monte Albán was founded around 500 B.C. by the Zapotec people. By about 220 B.C. it was a rich city, controlling nearby villages and towns. Hunters and farmers paid taxes and tributes, which supported rulers, priests, and scribes.

FARMERS AND BURIAL MOUNDS

AMERICAS

In North America, in cold or desert lands, many people lived as nomadic hunters and gatherers. But in other regions, such as the Ohio and Mississippi river valleys, the climate was mild and the land was fertile. The Adena people lived in villages and farmed the land around the Ohio River. They grew enough food to support a growing population. The Adena people were skilled builders and made huge mounds of earth where they buried their dead. Adena merchants traveled long distances to trade craft goods and food with other North Americans. They traded with the Hopewell people, farther northwest, who became rich and powerful after about 300 B.C.

NOMADIC LIFE

AUSTRALASIA

In the Pacific Ocean many of the major islands were inhabited by Alexander's time, although Hawaii and New Zealand had still not been discovered. There were no kingdoms, no cities, and perhaps no settled villages. Most people were nomads, living in temporary huts made of twigs, bark, and leaves. There are no written records and little evidence of how these societies were organized. But people adapted their lifestyle to their environment and sometimes may have fought over food and territory.

FAMOUS RULERS AND LEADERS

▲ General Pericles was leader of the Greek city-state of Athens from 461 to 429 B.C. People admired him for his wisdom and his success in war. He also encouraged music, plays, art, philosophy, and science. Athens became head of a powerful empire under his rule.

In Alexander the Great's day, most countries or states were ruled by a single person. A ruler could fight to win control of a whole empire and then stay in power for life, if he had the strongest and biggest army. Rulers like Alexander needed good advisors and army generals to help them rule but did not always take their advice. Rulers often dismissed advisors, or even had them murdered, if they became too powerful or had strong ideas of their own.

GREEK CITY-STATES

Greek city-states all had their own form of government. Some were ruled by families, and some, by groups of rich men. A few, like Macedonia, were ruled by kings. We know most about the city-state of Athens. It was an early kind of democracy. All adult male citizens had the right to choose their ruler, although women and slaves could not vote. Athenian citizens could help plan government policy by debating it at a public assembly. They could also serve as government officials and help make sure the law was carried out fairly. The Athenians disliked kingship and were proud of their system of democracy.

APPIUS CLAUDIUS

In Alexander's time, Rome was a republic. It was governed by two officials called consuls, who were elected every year. One of the most famous leaders was Appius Claudius, who was a clever general and politician. In 312 B.C. he changed the law to give ordinary people more power to give their point of view to the government. He also tried to improve everyday life in Rome. He commissioned the city's first aqueduct.

CELTIC CHIEFS

We do not know the names of any Celtic leaders who lived in Alexander the Great's time. But from ancient stories and songs, written down hundreds of years later, we know that the Celts valued strength and bravery. The most powerful chiefs were war leaders, but there was also a class of priest-lawkeepers called druids. Some Celtic heroes lived wild in the mountains and forests with groups of loyal warriors.

▲ Appius Claudius was responsible for Italy's first main road, called the Appian Way. It was begun in 312 B.C. and was built of stones, rubble, and lime mortar. It was important in linking Rome with its conquered cities.

◄ This stern-faced Celtic ruler lived in eastern Europe. A Celtic chieftain's duty was to lead his men in battle and enforce the law in the tribe.

CHANDRAGUPTA

SOUTH ASIA

Alexander the Great and his army marched away from India in 325 B.C. As soon as they had gone, a young Indian prince called Chandragupta Maurya wasted no time in planning how to seize power and build his own empire. He took his own private army to the north of India and conquered the kingdom of Magadha. He went on to attack the Macedonian governor, who was guarding Indian lands for Alexander, and won them for himself. By 322 B.C., the year after Alexander died, Chandragupta ruled all northern India and set up a new empire there. His descendants, called the Mauryas, conquered more land. By 232 B.C. they ruled an empire that stretched from the Himalaya Mountains to the far southern part of India.

ASOKA THE WISE

King Asoka of India was Chandragupta's grandson. He was also a mighty warrior. He conquered many new lands and almost doubled the empire's size. But after one battle, when more than 100,000 men were killed, Asoka realized how terrible war is. He became a follower of the Buddhist religion (see page 43) and worked to keep peace in his lands.

As a Buddhist, Asoka wanted to make life better for everyone in his empire. Most people there were farmers, but their crops often died from lack of rain. So Asoka built new reservoirs, dams, wells, and canals to bring water to their fields. He planted forests and shady roadside trees and built hospitals and resthouses for travelers. He planned new roads and new towns to promote trade.

In many parts of his empire, Asoka set up tall pillars carved with words and pictures about Buddhism. He built monasteries and monuments at Buddhist holy sites, and sent missionaries, including his own son and daughter, to teach people in many Asian lands about the Buddhist faith.

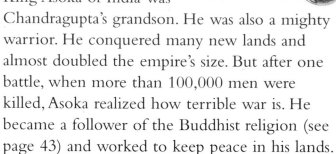

◄ Asoka set up special stone pillars throughout his empire. They were topped with carved lions, which were Asoka's symbol. The lions are balanced on four wheels, which are the symbols of Buddhist law.

RULING AN EMPIRE

The greatest Persian emperor was Darius I, who ruled from 522 to 486 B.C. He divided the empire into 20 small districts, so they would be easy to control. Each one was ruled by a governor called a satrap. The satraps were usually members of the Persian royal family or trustworthy friends. King Darius built himself a vast new palace and many roads, linking the far-flung corners of the empire with his capital city. He also built a canal that connected the Nile River to the Red Sea.

In the years after Darius I died, the Persian Empire was weakened by royal plots, rebellions, and civil wars.

▲ Darius III was defeated in three major battles against Alexander the Great. Here Darius is leading his army from a chariot at the Battle of Issus.

LOSING AN EMPIRE

King Darius III was the last Persian emperor. He ruled for only five years, until he was defeated by Alexander the Great's army at the Battle of Gaugamela in 331 B.C. Darius ran away to hide, but his own soldiers found him and murdered him. After this victory, Alexander burned the Persians' splendid palace at Persepolis to show that the Persian Empire had ended.

▲ About 520 B.C. King Darius I built a huge new palace at Persepolis, where he lived for a few weeks every year. The stairway was carved with portraits of people from many different parts of his empire. He ordered people from all over his empire to come to the palace and offer him gifts, as a sign that they were under his command.

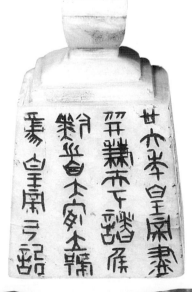

► A weight from the kingdom of Qin. It is made of a precious green stone called jade. Before Emperor Qin Shi Huangdi united the Chinese Empire, each Chinese state had its own different weights, measures, and coins.

TIGER EMPEROR

EAST ASIA

Prince Cheng of Qin was the first emperor of China. He ruled for 11 years, from 221 to 210 B.C. He was so cruel and fierce that he was given a nickname, the Tiger of Qin. He ordered his soldiers to burn all books he did not agree with. Scholars who protested were buried alive.

The emperor made strict new laws to help his empire run smoothly. He built roads and canals so that soldiers, merchants, and messengers could travel quickly from place to place. He introduced a standard style of handwriting and required government officials to wear black clothes. All carts and chariots had to have wheels exactly the same distance apart, so they could travel along rutted country roads. The emperor also forced ordinary people to serve in the army and to help build the Great Wall (see page 33). If they arrived late for duty, they were killed.

▲ Japanese legends say that the first emperor was the son of the sun goddess, Amaterasu, and that the other emperors were descended from her. They were honored as if they were gods.

POWERFUL WOMEN

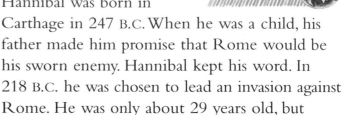

EAST ASIA

We do not know for certain the names of any Japanese rulers who lived in Alexander the Great's time. Ancient legends say there were four rulers between 475 and 158 B.C., called Kosho, Koan, Korei, and Kogen. Some historians think that Japan was ruled by powerful women from the Yayoi civilization. Yayoi rulers seem to have been peace-loving and devoted to religion and the arts, unlike later Japanese rulers, who respected warriors' skills above everything else.

► Hannibal spent his life fighting against Rome. In 183 B.C., when victory seemed impossible, he killed himself rather than surrender to Roman troops.

HANNIBAL

AFRICA

Hannibal was born in Carthage in 247 B.C. When he was a child, his father made him promise that Rome would be his sworn enemy. Hannibal kept his word. In 218 B.C. he was chosen to lead an invasion against Rome. He was only about 29 years old, but already a brilliant soldier—bold, brave, and clever.

For his invasion, Hannibal took a number of elephants and about 40,000 men. They marched through Spain and France and over the Alps, the mountains that defended Italy in the north. The journey was terrible—across steep mountain slopes and through freezing snow. Most of his elephants and about 14,000 men died on the way. But Hannibal would not give up. When he reached Italy, Roman soldiers marched north to defend their land, but Hannibal's army won battle after battle. Hannibal stayed in Italy for many years, fighting against Rome, but he never captured the city.

PTOLEMY I

When Alexander died, one of his generals, called Ptolemy, became governor of Egypt. Ptolemy spent the first half of his reign defending Egypt from attack by neighboring peoples and building up his own power. He declared himself King of Egypt in 305 B.C. and founded a new dynasty of kings and queens that ruled Egypt until 30 B.C. The last ruler in Ptolemy's dynasty was Queen Cleopatra. Ptolemy introduced Greek and Macedonian customs into his kingdom, and reorganized the Egyptian army like a Macedonian one. Greek became the official language.

MAYAN KINGS

AMERICAS

From about 200 B.C. the Maya were the most powerful people in Mexico and Central America. Maya kings and princes had to be bold battle commanders because Maya states were often at war. The Maya believed that their kings and queens were descended from the gods. They thought that holy blood flowed through their veins. At important religious ceremonies kings and queens had to make offerings of their blood in the temples, to ask the gods for help.

▲ Ptolemy I was a Macedonian, but in this statue, Egyptian sculptors have shown him as an Egyptian pharaoh.

CHIEFS AND COUNCILS

In many Native American groups in North America, there was a single leader, or chief. He was usually chosen because of his experience and special skills. But sometimes there was no one single ruler, and there were no royal families, where the right to be king was passed from father to son. Instead, important decisions were made by a council of men, and possibly women, who had won the respect of the community for their intelligence, bravery, or wealth.

EXPLORERS

AUSTRALASIA

We do not know the names of any powerful people who lived in Australia or the Pacific Islands in Alexander the Great's time. But Pacific peoples must have admired the adventurers and explorers who set sail in canoes across the vast ocean, hoping to find land where their families could settle and begin a new life. In Australia, leaders who could find water in the desert, invent new traps to catch fish and birds, or make contact with the spirits in dances and dreams would all have won respect.

► Little clay figures like this were often buried in early Maya tombs. No one knows exactly why they were made, but they may show the ancestors of powerful leaders, or guardians to keep evil spirits away.

HOW PEOPLE LIVED

In Alexander the Great's day, most people lived very simple lives. Their homes were small, with only one or two rooms. They were built of local materials, such as rough stone, wood and thatch, or mudbrick. They had no gas, electricity, or clean water supplies.

Ordinary people wore simple clothes, woven from wool or plant fibers such as cotton or linen, or made from animal skins. They ate simple foods, like grains and vegetables, which they grew themselves or bought in local markets. Life was different for a few rich people. Kings and queens, nobles, army commanders, top government officials, and leading merchants had the biggest, safest, and most comfortable homes, the finest clothes, and the best food.

▲ This vase shows Greek farmers harvesting olives. Olives were one of the most important crops in Greece. They were crushed to make oil, which was used for cooking, for burning in lamps, and to soften people's skin.

FARMING AND FISHING

EUROPE

In many parts of southern Europe, farmers grazed sheep and goats on wild mountain pastures and grew barley, grapes, and olives in sheltered valleys. Fishermen sailed out to sea to catch tuna, octopus, and squid. Men also hunted deer and wild boar in the woods. Women gathered herbs, fruits, and nuts; kept chickens; and made cheese.

THE BIG CITY

There were few cities in Europe, but Rome was probably one of the biggest. Ordinary people lived crowded together in small huts and blocks of flats. They worked at crafts and trades, making metal goods, pottery, woollen cloth, furniture, and leather boots and shoes. Some merchants traded luxury goods such as amber and perfumes from Arabia or slaves from Africa. Other traders sold bread, fruit and vegetables, or such foods as pies, stew, and soup, from market stalls.

▼ The streets of Rome were lined with craft workers' stalls. This stone carving shows a coppersmith's workshop. You can see his goods for sale, his workbench, and some of his tools.

▲ This photograph shows a modern reconstruction of a Celtic farmhouse. It is built of strong wooden poles. The walls are made of woven twigs covered with mud or clay, called wattle and daub. The roof is covered with a thick thatch of dried grass or straw.

ROUND HOUSES

In Celtic lands people built big round houses made out of wood and mud. Some villages were built on stilts, or on islands people made in the middle of a lake, for defense. Enemy skulls were often hung over doorways, to keep evil spirits away.

Celtic farmers planted crops of wheat, oats, and barley and kept cattle, sheep, and goats. Women wore long robes, while men wore short tunics and baggy trousers tied at the ankle. Men and women wore cloaks made of checked cloth. They often bleached their hair, using wood ash and urine. Before a battle, men painted their bodies with magic patterns, using blue ink made from plants.

RICH PERSIAN CITIES

MIDDLE EAST

When Alexander conquered Persia, he took over one of the richest empires in the world. Nobles and families working for the government had houses full of rich treasures, given as tribute from rulers of nearby lands. Persian merchants who crossed the Arabian desert with caravans of camels also had valuable goods to sell. They arrived at bustling market towns with perfumes, incense, gold jewelry, and pearls. Fine horses from Assyria and cattle from Mesopotamia were sold there, too. Craft workers sold silver drinking cups, furs, leather saddles and bridles, and weapons of many kinds.

Cities in the Persian Empire were supported by the hard work of slaves and by farm goods brought in from the countryside. Farmers grew barley to make bread, sesame seeds for their oil, almonds, and figs. They kept flocks of sheep with valuable silky fleece.

VILLAGE LIFE

SOUTH ASIA

In India most people lived in villages and worked on the land. In the warm, rainy South, farmers planted fields of cotton and harvested mangoes and coconuts. In the cooler, drier North, they kept cows and grew barley and wheat. In cold mountain villages farmers kept sheep and goats and planted orchards of apricot trees, which were introduced from Persia during Alexander the Great's time.

RICE AND ELEPHANTS

In Southeast Asia the main crop was rice. Houses were made of wooden poles, roofed with leaves or grass. They were often built on stilts to protect them from floods caused by tropical rains. Villagers trained elephants to carry tree trunks from the forests to use for building. We know about these villages, because craft workers made beautiful bronze drums with pictures of houses and scenes of daily life on them.

▶ These multistory houses in the town of Sanaa, in present-day Yemen, were built in Alexander's day, though they have been repaired and redecorated many times since then. Towns in Arabia grew rich through long-distance trade.

▲ Chinese farmers moved heavy loads of grain or straw in bullock carts. This model cart was made to be buried alongside a dead farmer in his tomb.

FORCED TO FARM

EAST ASIA

Around 350 B.C. a scholar called Lord Shang became a chief advisor in the kingdom of Qin. He told the government to encourage farming and crafts. That way, he said, the people of Qin would grow strong and healthy, because they would be warmly clothed and well-fed. The government could collect taxes on the food and goods people produced. These taxes would pay for a bigger army and lots of weapons to help Qin conquer more land.

Lord Shang ordered all people except craft workers, farmers, and soldiers to leave their jobs. Instead they had to work at useful tasks in the countryside making farm tools, digging irrigation ditches, weaving cloth, building walls of pounded earth to protect the villages, raising animals, and growing crops.

Many people were unhappy at being forced to farm, but Lord Shang's plan succeeded. The state of Qin grew rich and strong. By 221 B.C. it had conquered all other states in China.

A TRADER'S LIIFE

AFRICA

The Phoenician city of Carthage was a large, bustling port. It had two harbors. One was used by the navy. The second, bigger harbor was used by merchant ships. It was surrounded by warehouses where merchants stored their goods. There were also workshops, staffed by skilled artisans, where new ships were built and old ships could be repaired.

Some merchants became very rich. They wore fine robes of silk and wool and paid for stone and ivory carvings to decorate their houses. They ate good food: bread, meat, fresh fruit, and wine.

▼ Phoenician traders sailed all around the Mediterranean Sea in ships like this one. Ships were made of wood and had a wide hull to carry lots of cargo. They were powered by sail, and by oar when there was no wind. They were steered by a big oar at the rear, as shown below.

DATES AND YAMS

AFRICA

In many parts of Africa, there were peoples who worked in metals and farmed the land. In areas with good rainfall, farmers cleared fields from tropical forests and grew yams and plantains. They gathered wild fruits and insect grubs from the forests and fished in the wide, crocodile-infested rivers. In the city of Meroë, people lived in houses made of mudbrick. They ate meat, grains, and dates and wore clothes made of wool and flax. Rich people wore jewelry made of gold and ivory.

▶ In Egypt, girls helped their mothers prepare food and weave cloth. Boys worked with their fathers on the farm. But Egyptian children still had time to play. This wooden doll with long curly hair, made about 500 B.C., was found in a tomb.

HUNTING AND HERDING

Peoples in the dry regions of Africa made a living by herding cattle. Some African peoples also hunted lions, leopards, elephants, and antelope for furs, ivory, or meat. They used arrows tipped with stone or sharpened bone, sometimes dipped in poison. Their houses were made of earth, thatched with leaves or grass. Some people hunted in the Sahara in horse-drawn chariots and camped at wadis.

FLOODED LAND

Egyptian people believed in life after death. So they decorated their tombs with paintings of activities they had enjoyed while they were alive. There were pictures of boating, feasting, and listening to music. They buried useful tools and favorite possessions in their tombs, too, to take with them to the world of the dead. Tomb paintings tell us that the land of Egypt was just right for growing wheat, grapes, figs, melons, and many tasty vegetables. Lush grass grew there, too, providing food for sheep, cows, and goats. The fertile soil was created by the Nile River floods. Every year the waters spread over the land, leaving a layer of rich black mud.

TERRACED FIELDS

AMERICAS

The high Andes Mountains, which run along the western coast of South America, make up one of the most difficult environments in the world. The weather is bitterly cold, the air is thin, and the soil is poor and stony. People cut terraces into the mountain slopes to hold soil in place. Here they grew potatoes and corn. They made irrigation ditches to bring water from melted glaciers to help their crops grow. They had no iron or steel, so they dug their fields with wooden sticks. There were no tall trees to provide wood for building, so they made their homes from rough blocks of stone.

The women combed fine, silky hair from sheeplike animals called llamas and alpacas and spun it into thread, which they wove into cloth. The most beautiful cloth was made to wrap mummies in before they were buried.

LOCAL LIFESTYLES

There were many other kinds of environments in North and South America—from the icy Arctic to the thick woodlands of the Northeast, the hot deserts of Mexico, and the steamy tropical rain forests of the Amazon. By Alexander's time they had all been settled by different native peoples. Each had discovered a way of life that was suited to the local climate, plants, and wildlife.

▼ The Paracas people, who lived in the Andes, were expert weavers. They made cloth with beautiful patterns, using more than 100 different shades of color. They made their dyes from plants and crushed earth. The cloth below was made by Paracas women about 500 B.C.

▲ In the icy Arctic regions of North America, Inuit women used sharp knives like this one, made of slate, to cut up seals that hunters had killed. Their families ate the meat and fat, and then the women scraped the skins clean and used them to make clothing.

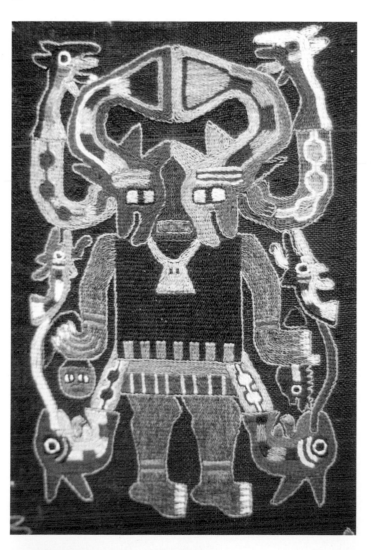

SURVIVAL SKILLS

AUSTRALASIA

The Aborigines of Australia continued to develop hunting skills that were thousands of years old. Men made nets and traps to catch wild birds, eels, and fish. They covered themselves with mud to hide their human scent before stalking kangaroos and killing them with boomerangs and spears. Women gathered seeds and berries and used sticks to dig for roots. They could dig enough food for a day in about two hours. Scientists have now discovered that these roots are full of vitamins.

► The Aborigines hunted and trapped wild animals. This Aborigine rock painting shows a hunter and a kangaroo. People may have made these paintings to give them power over the animals they drew.

DISCOVERY AND INVENTION

Before Alexander the Great's time, farmers and builders invented new tools and developed new ways of working to help them grow better crops or build bigger buildings. Craft workers discovered how to make finer cloth and stronger pottery and weapons. New materials and new techniques were usually discovered by chance, or because of a single clever idea. This made the pace of change unpredictable.

Then, around 500 B.C., a whole new way of inventing and discovering began. People in Greece and Greek lands in the Middle East discovered by first-hand observations important scientific principles. They used this knowledge to try to understand the world around them—how our bodies work, why the sun rises and sets, and what everything is made of. Because of their research, historians call the Greeks the world's first scientists.

▲ Aristotle was Alexander's tutor, and the greatest scientist and philosopher in Greece. He discovered things by careful study and measurement and by understanding the laws that govern the way the world works. For example, he introduced classifications, showing how plants and animals could be sorted into groups.

WORLD DISCOVERY

EUROPE

Greek explorers made important discoveries about the world. They visited Europe, Africa, and Asia. But Greek geographers also figured out that there were probably other lands that had not yet been discovered. (Australia and the Americas were both unknown to them.) Greek astronomers also figured out that the earth must be round, not flat, because the earth cast a curved shadow across the moon during an eclipse.

GREEK DOCTORS

Greek doctors made important discoveries in medicine. They examined their patients and asked them about their lifestyle. They found out that the wrong food, a dirty environment, and even a person's state of mind could all cause disease. They kept records of their treatments, so they could find out which worked best. They cut up dead bodies to find out what caused disease, so they could care better for their patients.

▲ The Romans were skillful builders and engineers. This tombstone, probably made for a family of builders, shows a building site with a big hoist, used for lifting heavy loads.

BUILDERS AND ENGINEERS

The Romans were less theoretical than the Greeks, but by careful trial and error they made several important advances in building design. They built good roads, strong walls to protect their city, and long, arched aqueducts to bring fresh water from faraway mountain streams. They dug huge sewers underneath the city to carry away dirty water and human waste. Around 200 B.C. they invented the world's first concrete, using lime, water, and volcanic ash.

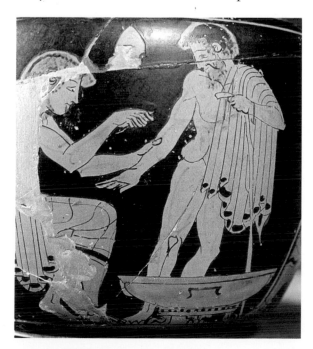

◄ This vase, made around 400 B.C., shows a Greek doctor examining a patient's arm. Greek doctors studied the way the body is made. Sometimes they cut up dead bodies to find out about muscles and bones beneath the skin.

▲ Babylonians kept records of what they saw on clay tablets, like this neatly written calendar, made around 400 B.C. They had invented their calendar by 2000 B.C. It divided days into 24 hours and hours into 60 minutes.

MEASURING TIME

MIDDLE EAST

Babylonians were world leaders in astronomy. Every night priests and astronomers climbed to the top of tall ziggurats to watch and record the movements of the moon and the stars. They also studied the hours of sunrise and sunset and the changing seasons. Around 340 B.C. an astronomer called Kidenas discovered that for two days each year, in spring and autumn, day and night are of equal length all round the world. These are called equinoxes, which means "equal nights."

HOROSCOPES

The first-known personal horoscopes were made in Babylon about 400 B.C. Astronomers worked out the position of the stars at a baby's birth and used this information to predict the person's future. People made important decisions based on horoscopes. People in other parts of the world also believed that feelings and actions could be influenced by the sun, moon, and stars.

FAMOUS SCHOOLS

SOUTH ASIA

Indian schools were famous in Asia and as far away as the Middle East. There were hundreds of small forest schools in India, on the edge of busy towns. Each was run by a single teacher. There was also an ancient university at Taxila, in the far northwest of India. It was an honor to win a place at the university, and students from many Asian lands traveled vast distances to study there. Mathematicians and doctors trained at Taxila were especially skilled.

WAR ELEPHANTS

There were many military experts in India who designed new swords and spears from the strongest and best-quality steel, which Indian blacksmiths had recently discovered how to make. They also trained horses and elephants to fight in wars. Indian war elephants were a terrifying, deadly weapon.

▲ This Greek coin shows Indian war elephants used in fighting Alexander's troops. The elephants in the Indian army had metal tips fitted to their tusks.

CHINESE INVENTIONS

EAST ASIA

By around 300 B.C., Chinese engineers were using iron to make gates and bridges, as well as farm tools and weapon. Chinese inventors also designed the first crossbow fired by pulling a trigger and invented poison gas. To encourage these and other inventions, Chinese ruler Prince Xuan founded a college for scientists in 318 B.C.

CHINESE MEDICINE

Around 200 B.C., Chinese scholars wrote a book called *The Book of Medicine of the Yellow Emperor*. It described important medical treatments that had been developed over the previous 500 years. The Chinese did not operate on people. They believed that people could be well only if the whole body were treated, not just the injured or sick part. Many of the remedies, such as herbal medicines and acupuncture, are still used today.

THE EMPEROR'S WALL

When Prince Cheng won control of China in 221 B.C., one of his most urgent tasks was to defend his new lands. In about 214 B.C. he sent one of his generals to the northern frontier, with orders to build a Great Wall. Remains of earlier walls were there already, but this was to be bigger and stronger than anything before.

The Great Wall of China was an impressive engineering achievement. Thousands of peasants and soldiers worked in the cold and wet to build the wall out of pounded earth and thick stone slabs. When completed, it was about 1,500 miles long and averaged 30 feet high, with a road about 6 feet wide running along the top. It has been rebuilt many times since then.

▼ The Great Wall is an amazing achievement. But so many workers died building it and were buried in the wall's foundations that it has been called the world's biggest tomb.

SCIENCE CITY

AFRICA

The city of Alexandria, on the northern coast of Egypt, was founded in 332 B.C. by Alexander the Great. It soon became a great center of learning and a rich trading port. By 300 B.C. the world's first museum was built there. This was a spendid study center, where scholars from many lands could meet to research subjects such as science and astronomy, and to discuss the latest ideas.

Next a magnificent library was started by ruler Ptolemy I. The library held copies of all the most important Greek and Middle Eastern scientific, mathematical, and medical texts, carefully copied out by hand on over 700,000 papyrus scrolls.

THE LIGHTHOUSE

In 283 B.C. workers started to build a huge lighthouse at the entrance to Alexandria's two harbors. It was about 390 feet high and topped with a fire that was kept burning all the time. Horses pulled cartloads of firewood up sloping ramps, right to the top of the tower. Light from the fire was reflected by huge metal mirrors and could been seen by sailors miles out from the shore. It helped them steer a safe course.

◄ The lighthouse at Alexandria was the world's most famous lighthouse. It stood for about 1,500 years but has now completely disappeared. You can see a picture of it on this Greek coin.

METALWORKING

The kingdoms of Meroë and Nok were centers of ironworking. Their craft workers were among the first people in Africa to discover how to make iron, hundreds of years before Alexander's time. It was an important discovery. Iron was tough, but it could be molded or hammered into different shapes. It was ideal for weapons and tools for farming. The raw materials, wood and iron ore, were all around. Ironworkers built big dome-shaped clay ovens where they burned crushed iron ore at a high temperature, until the iron in the ore melted and ran out.

Meroë craft workers were also skilled gold workers. They engraved patterns on the surface of gold using a pointed tool. Sometimes they hammered out a pattern from the back, to created a raised picture.

▲ Meroë gold workers made cups, dishes, and plaques with detailed scenes. This gold plaque shows a Meroë king worshiping a hawk-headed god.

MAYA MATH

Most native peoples of the Americas did not know how to read and write. But around 400 B.C. the Zapotecs began to use a system of little pictures, called glyphs, to keep written records. No one has yet been able to work out what they mean.

The Maya also wrote using glyphs (which archaeologists have learned to read). They used them to keep records, such as the number of captives taken in war. Scribes also kept a calendar, which they used to work out the dates of religious festivals. The Maya did not invent this calendar, but they revised and perfected it. It continued to be used for over 1,000 years. The Maya also invented a way of counting, based on three symbols: a shell for zero, a dot for one, and a bar for five.

▲ Maya scribes made thousands of folding books with picture writing, called codexes. They were written with colored inks on paper made from fig-tree bark. The only ones to survive were made long after Alexander's time. The one above shows part of a calendar.

MOUND BUILDERS

Hundreds of earth mounds built by the Adena and Hopewell peoples still survive in North America. Many have been destroyed by farmers or buried under towns. Mounds were used as sacred enclosures or as burial sites for important people. Hundreds of workers dug the earth with simple sticks and shovels and carried it to the mound site. They had no horses or wheeled vehicles to help them. They did not know how to smelt rocks and minerals to make iron and bronze, so all their tools were made of stone. Inside the mounds, tombs were built as small clay-lined pits, or as bigger houses made of logs.

► This Hopewell knife is made of a hard stone called quartz. It has been carefully shaped to create a very sharp edge. The finest knives were made to display—they were too valuable or everyday use.

PACIFIC DISCOVERY

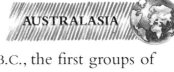

Between 500 and 300 B.C., the first groups of settlers began to arrive on remote Pacific islands from Fiji, Tonga, and Samoa. They traveled in canoes that were fast and designed to be stable in the rough sea. They were powered by sails woven from palm-leaf fibers, and steered by a single wooden oar. The hulls were hollowed from tree trunks by burning, soaking, and scraping. Ropes were twisted from coconut fiber, which was waterproof and strong. The settlers had to learn new skills to survive. They had to discover the best materials and sites to build their homes and which animals and plants they could safely eat.

THE CREATIVE WORLD

For Alexander, and for many other people living in his time, art had a special purpose. It showed people how important and rich kings and princes were or gave honor to the gods. Buildings, statues, and objects had to look beautiful, but simple decoration was not enough. Most designs and styles had a meaning. To add to his image as a strong man, Alexander chose to be painted and sculpted looking like the legendary Greek hero Hercules.

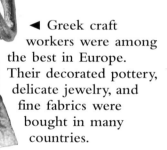

◀ Greek craft workers were among the best in Europe. Their decorated pottery, delicate jewelry, and fine fabrics were bought in many countries.

▲ The gold earrings above and above right were made in Greece around 330 B.C. Like many other objects at this time, they are a mixture of Greek and Asian design.

NEW STYLES

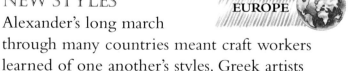

EUROPE

Alexander's long march through many countries meant craft workers learned of one another's styles. Greek artists borrowed ideas and techniques from other lands, and their designs became more complicated. At the same time, artists in Asia and the Middle East learned the Greek style from the cities Alexander built and the things his army took with them. Greek designs became mixed with local styles to produce a new style called Hellenistic.

▲ Celtic chieftains would have used decorated bronze wine jugs like these at great feasts.

THE BEST OF GREECE

When Alexander marched into Greece in 335 B.C., one of the first things he did was to destroy the city of Thebes, as a warning to all Greeks to surrender. Thebes, like other Greek cities, had many temples, theaters, sports arenas, and public squares, full of beautiful statues, carvings, and mosaics. Most had been built during the previous 100 years, when Greek city-states were growing rich and strong. In Athens there were many new buildings at this time, including a temple called the Parthenon. It was made of white marble and held a sculpture in ivory and gold of the goddess Athena. It was designed as a war memorial.

▼ The royal palace at Susa was decorated with pictures like the one below, made of tiles and glazed bricks. Clay bricks were colored with glazes made of crushed rocks, salt, and powdered clay, then baked in a special oven to make a thin, shiny surface.

CELTIC PATTERNS

Celtic craft workers in Britain and France decorated cups, mirrors, weapons, and jewelry made of iron, bronze, silver, and gold. In southern England, they carved huge figures of guardian gods and magic animals into chalky hillsides, to bring good luck. Celtic patterns were curved and swirling. They were often based on plant or animal shapes. Sometimes they showed gods and magic beasts. Celtic craft workers also copied designs from nearby peoples, such as the Greeks and Etruscans.

PERSIAN PALACES

MIDDLE EAST

There were many great buildings in the Persian cities. The palace at Persepolis had a vast royal hall, held up by a forest of carved stone columns. At Susa the palace walls were decorated with friezes of men, monsters, and gods. Babylon was the most spectacular city of all, with a huge royal palace and a great temple. A road called the Grand Processional Way led to the temple. It was decorated with lions, flowers, and patterns made of glazed and colored bricks.

EMPIRE OF NOMADS

MIDDLE EAST

In Alexander's time a group of nomads called the Scythians formed an empire on the borders of the Middle East and eastern Europe. They may even have fought against the Macedonians. They were fierce warriors, who made drinking cups from the skulls of their enemies. As nomads they had to carry their belongings with them. They traded with the Greeks, who made objects for them, but their own artisans also made beautifully decorated swords and ornaments, as well as armor made of metal scales. One Scythian woman has been found, preserved in ice, wearing gold bracelets and gold rings on every finger.

▼ A Scythian artisan made this gold vase. It is decorated with pictures of warriors and their weapons. Scythian artists were especially skilled at working with fine leather, furs, and gold.

A ROYAL PALACE

SOUTH ASIA

In India, Chandragupta built a new capital city at Pataliputra. It stretched for 9 miles along the side of the Ganges River and was surrounded by strong wooden walls with 64 gates and 570 watchtowers. People said the palace was more splendid than anything in the Persian Empire. The king employed craft workers and artists from Greece, Persia, and India. At the palace, dancers and actors would have performed songs and poems, such as the *Mahabharata*, to entertain and educate the court.

▲ King Asoka built this stupa at Sanchi, in central India. It is covered with roughly shaped stone blocks.

THE ART OF ASOKA

King Asoka wanted to fill India with buildings and monuments dedicated to his new-found Buddhist faith. He paid the very best Indian artists and craft workers to build tombs for holy men, and stupas (dome-shaped monuments) at Buddhist holy places. According to legend, he gave orders for 84,000 stupas to be built. Indian woodworkers and stonecarvers decorated these important buildings with graceful and lifelike carvings of people, animals, and plants.

▲ One of Qin Shi Huangdi's terra-cotta soldiers. The statues were brightly painted with paints made from minerals bound with animal blood or egg white, and charcoal for the hair. But over the years most of the paint has faded or flaked away.

TERRA-COTTA ARMY

EAST ASIA

In 1974, Chinese archaeologists found an army of life-size terra-cotta warriors, buried underground (see page 14). They had been put there to guard the tomb of Qin Shi Huangdi, the first Chinese emperor. In earlier years real soldiers would have been buried with their dead lord.

The soldiers' bodies and arms were made from coils of wet clay, and the heads and hands were made separately in molds. The face of each soldier was covered in a layer of clay so that each one could be given his own character. All the details of his uniform and weapons were carefully copied. The clay was then fired. About 700,000 workers took 36 years to prepare the tomb.

JAPANESE POTTERY

For hundreds of years the Jomon people of Japan had made pots and statues out of coils of clay, shaped by hand. They decorated their work with rope-like patterns and with small scrolls and spiral designs. But around 300 B.C. the Yayoi people taught them how to make finer, more delicate pottery using a potter's wheel. They also taught them how to make iron and bronze and to use it for fine weapons, jewelry, and bells.

SUIT OF JADE

Chinese artists made beautiful statues and dishes of bronze and of glazed, painted pottery. They made combs, boxes, and cups of shiny lacquer. Lacquer is made from layers of hard-dried sap from an oriental tree. Craft workers carved statues and jewelry out of a precious green stone called jade. The Chinese believed that jade had special powers to protect their souls and bodies from evil. For this reason, people were often buried with jade objects alongside them.

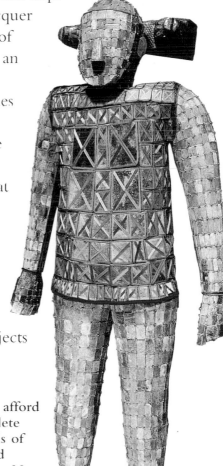

▶ Rich people could afford to be buried in complete suits of jade. Hundreds of jade squares were held together by gold wires. No complete suit has survived from Alexander's time. This one was made about 200 years later.

MEROË, THE KINGDOM OF GOLD

AFRICA

Ever since Ancient Egyptian times, the peoples of Kush and Meroë had supplied tributes of gold as peace offerings to Egyptian pharaohs. By Alexander's time the kings who ruled Kush had become powerful enough to keep the gold for themselves. They employed expert craft workers to make beautiful gold objects, such as cups, plaques, and even containers for reed pens. Around 300 B.C. the kings of Kush moved to live in the city of Meroë. They built many fine new palaces and temples there. Architects, stonecarvers, and builders mixed designs copied from Greek and Egyptian buildings with local African styles, to create a bold, new style of their own.

▼ This massive gateway at the entrance to a temple near the city of Meroë was built around 330 B.C. The stone has crumbled with age, but there are traces of Greek decoration at the top of the columns on either side of the door.

WORKING WITH CLAY

In West Africa the Nok people skillfully molded clay into lifelike statues of people and animals. Some of the craft work is so detailed that archaeologists can use it to discover what clothes and jewelry people wore, and even how they plaited their hair. In East Africa, people from the Chifumbaze civilization were skilled ironworkers and potters. They made molded and decorated bowls and pots.

▶ This statue of an elephant was made sometime between 500 and 200 B.C. Because the Nok people left no written records, we do not know if they made figures like this for religious reasons or simply as ornaments.

POTTERY AND CLOTH

AMERICAS

In South America the Paracas people made beautiful textiles, woven from cotton, and embroidered in brilliant colors (see page 29). They also made fine pottery, decorated with birds' heads or human faces. The finest pottery was buried alongside mummies. After about 370 B.C. the Nazca people of Peru also began to make fine textiles. They were often decorated with real feathers. They made pottery, which they glazed in six or seven different colors.

◄ The Great Serpent Mound, in southern Ohio, was built by the Adena-Hopewell people. It is made of hard-packed earth and is more than 1,300 feet from open jaws to tail. The people believed that snakes had magic powers.

GREAT SERPENT MOUND

In North America, native peoples of the Adena and Hopewell civilizations built huge earthworks on top of burial sites or to mark sacred sites. The largest, the Great Serpent Mound, is more than 1,300 feet long. It was made in the shape of a snake swallowing an egg. Craft workers made simple pottery and carved beads, pendants, and tobacco pipes out of hard, shiny stone. They bought copper from peoples farther north to make rings, necklaces, and bracelets. Copper was much softer to work, and the decorations could be more detailed.

ART AND GODS

AUSTRALASIA

In many different parts of Australia, the Aborigines painted magical scenes in caves and on rocks, showing ancestor figures and wild animals or people hunting and dancing. Mostly they used colored earth for paint, but sometimes they carved their designs into the surface of the rock, using a sharp stone.

In the Pacific Islands, craft workers carved statues of mountain gods and sea spirits out of wood or plaited them from natural fibers, such as palm leaves. They often added prows carved in dramatic designs to the front of their canoes.

▼ This carving shows an ancestor spirit holding a spirit bird. It was carved to fit onto the prow of a war canoe. It was made in the nineteenth century, but it is based on a traditional design. People in the Pacific believed that the bird would keep the boat on the right course.

BELIEFS AND IDEAS

M any questions puzzled people living in Alexander's time. What made rain fall and crops grow? Why did floods and earthquakes happen? What was the right way for people to live? Mostly the answers were religious. People thought that everything was controlled by gods or goddesses, who demanded good behavior and gifts in return for their help.

From about 500 B.C. Greek and Egyptian scholars had begun to look for scientific reasons to explain why things happened. But ideas took time to become accepted. When one astronomer said that the sun was not a god, he was punished by the law courts of Athens, even though Pericles tried to defend him.

▲ This gold plaque was made as an offering to the Persian god Ahura Mazda. The priest is carrying a bundle of wood, called barsom rods, to feed the holy fire. Fire rituals were carried out to help the power of good in the battle against evil.

OLYMPIC GAMES

EUROPE

In Greece many people still believed in the old gods and goddesses. They built temples and statues in their honor and made offerings of food and wine. They went to ask oracles for advice. They took part in religious processions, with music, dancing and sports, and drama festivals, too. The Olympic Games was one of the most famous of these. It began in 776 B.C. as part of a festival in honor of Zeus, king of the gods, and continued for over a thousand years.

▲ The Greeks and the Romans worshiped many gods and goddesses. Each one looked after a different part of life. Athena was a wise warrior goddess. This is part of a temple built in her honor at Delphi, in Greece.

MOUNTAINS, LAKES, AND BONE FIRES

In Celtic lands people worshiped nature gods, who lived in mountains, forests, and lakes. At certain times of the year, such as midsummer, the Celts made human sacrifices. Victims were thrown into rivers and peat bogs, or burned. Our word *bonfire* comes from "bone fire."

ZOROASTER AND YAHWEH

MIDDLE EAST

In Persia most people followed the teachings of a holy man called Zoroaster. He lived around 600 B.C. and founded a new religion, based on the worship of Ahura Mazda, the god of goodness, truth, and light. The faith was led by priests, or wise men, called magi. After Alexander led his army through Persia, Zoroaster's teachings spread to many nearby lands.

In Canaan and Judah, the Jewish people worshiped their god, Yahweh. For hundreds of years many Jews had been kept as slaves in Babylon, until they were given their freedom in 538 B.C. by the Persian ruler, Cyrus the Great.

THE BUDDHA

SOUTH ASIA

In India most people followed the ancient Hindu religion. But by Alexander's time, many Indian people were also becoming followers of Siddhartha Gautama, known as the Buddha. The Buddha was an Indian prince, who lived some time between 560 and 480 B.C. Because all the suffering he saw in the world made him sad, he left his comfortable home and spent nearly six years meditating. He taught his followers that they should live unselfish lives, because this was the only way to end suffering in the world.

▶ When Alexander marched into India, he learned about Buddhist beliefs. He chose not to follow them, but many of the people he left behind accepted Buddhist ideas. This head of the Buddha was made around 400 or 300 B.C.

CONFUCIUS AND DAOISM

EAST ASIA

Confucius was born in China about 551 B.C. Although he believed in traditional ancestor-worship, he thought that this was not enough. He believed people needed to be taught how to live good lives. Confucius and his followers ran schools to teach his ideas to government officials, teachers, and other people who had the power to influence society.

At about the same time, a group of hermits criticized Confucius for thinking too much about society. Lao Zi, who probably lived between 400 and 300 B.C., wrote his ideas in a book. He told people to look for a way to live at peace with nature. His followers became known as Daoists, which means people seeking a peaceful way. Daoists see the world as a balance between dark and light forces, called yin and yang.

▲ Egyptian craft workers built massive statues to the gods and huge temples to house them, using ancient designs. This is the temple of Horus, the hawk-headed god of wisdom, built at Idfu, around 200 B.C.

◀ Confucius's good advice, which he hoped would guide people through their lives, was collected by his pupils and written down in books and scrolls.

GODS AND SPIRITS

AFRICA

Egyptian religion was 3,000 years old by Alexander's time. People in Egypt and nearby areas such as Meroë said prayers and made offerings to ancient Egyptian gods. These included Horus, the hawk-headed sky god; Bes, the god with a crown of feathers who protected women and children; and Anubis, the jackal-headed guardian of the dead.

In many parts of Africa, people believed that all living creatures and some nonliving things, such as statues, carvings, and royal jewels, were the home of spirits. African priests and people carried out special ceremonies, with chanting, drumming, and dancing, to welcome good spirits and drive bad ones away.

MOTHER EARTH

In North America many Native Americans shared similar beliefs. They honored the earth and tried to live in harmony with the natural world. Before cutting down a tree to make a house or killing a buffalo for food, they would apologize for the harm they were about to do and ask the tree or buffalo to forgive them.

► Native peoples in North and South America believed that magic healers and priests, called shamans, could communicate with the spirit world through prayers, music, and dancing. This pottery figure of a shaman was made in Mexico about 200 B.C.

SHAMANS AND SUN GODS

In Mexico and Central America, the Olmec and Maya worshiped animal gods, including fierce alligators and sharks. Some gods, such as were-jaguars, were half animal, half human. In South America, worshipers also prayed to the sun. They held festivals and offered sacrifices of people or human blood to the sun and to other nature gods. They believed their offerings would feed the gods and in return, the gods would make their crops and livestock grow.

SPIRIT POWER

In Australia, Aborigines believed in the Dreamtime. This was a time when the ancestors of all living creatures wandered across the land. They created the mountains, valleys, rivers, and deserts. When they had finished, they disappeared into the sky or turned into parts of the land. The Aborigines hoped to meet the spirits through dancing and music, because they believed the spirits still had power to guide them.

In the Pacific Ocean, islanders made statues of gods who controlled dangerous natural forces such as volcanoes and storms at sea. To please the gods, the islanders killed pigs, which were among their most valuable possessions. They put them on tall wooden platforms as presents for the gods.

▼ Many ancient holy sites, such as this water hole, are still used for Aborigine religious ceremonies.

PEOPLES FROM AROUND THE WORLD

Aborigines The first inhabitants of Australia, who arrived there about 40,000 years ago.

Adena People who lived in the Ohio Valley in North America from around 700 B.C. to A.D. 400. They were farmers and built huge burial mounds.

Celts Hunters and farmers who lived in northern Europe.

Chifumbaze The name given to people who lived in East Africa from around 500 B.C. They farmed and made iron and pottery goods.

Etruscans People who lived in northern Italy. They were powerful from around 800 to 200 B.C.

Hopewell A civilization that developed from the earlier Adena civilization (see above) from around 200 B.C. to A.D. 700. They were craft workers, traders, and mound builders.

Inuit Native Americans who arrived in the Arctic regions of North America from Siberia around 2000 B.C.

Jomon The name given to hunter-gatherers who lived in Japan from about 2500 to 300 B.C.

Maya A civilization in southern Mexico and Central America, most powerful from about A.D. 250 to 900. But the Maya were already building temples and other buildings and living in organized societies by 300 B.C.

Nabateans An Arab tribe of the Middle East that became rich and powerful around 400 B.C.

Native Americans The first inhabitants of America, who arrived about 30,000 years ago. Native American people were divided into many groups.

Nazca People who lived in southern Peru from about 200 B.C. to A.D. 600. Their civilization continued many of the traditions of the Paracas people (see below).

Olmecs The people who lived in the coastal forests of southern Mexico from around 2000 B.C.

Pacific peoples People who lived on islands in the Pacific Ocean.

Paracas People who lived on the southern coast of Peru from about 600 to 400 B.C. They were skilled textile workers and potters.

Phoenicians People who lived along the eastern Mediterranean coast. From around 1100 B.C. they built up a rich trading empire.

Scythians Nomads who lived on the shores of the Black Sea from around 600 to 300 B.C.

Yayoi People from Korea and northern China who went to live in Japan around 300 B.C.

Zapotecs People who lived in Mexico about 500 B.C. to A.D. 900.

acupuncture A form of medicine in which needles are pressed into the skin to treat illnesses.

aqueduct A raised channel, built to carry water.

archaeologist A person who studies the ancient past by digging up remains, such as bones or coins.

architect Someone who designs buildings.

astronomer Someone who studies the stars and planets.

Buddha A name for Gautama Siddhartha, a prince who lived in India in the sixth century B.C. He founded the religion of Buddhism.

burial mound A heap of earth used to cover and protect a grave.

citizens People who live in a city and often have a say in how it is run.

city-state A city or town, together with the surrounding villages and farms.

civilization A society with its own laws, customs, beliefs, and artistic traditions.

civil war War between different groups of people within the same country.

colony A group of people who settle in a country far from their homeland but keep ties with it.

commission To give orders and pay for something to be made.

coppersmith A craft worker who makes items out of copper.

democracy A system of government that allows citizens to make decisions about how their country should be governed.

dynasty A series of rulers belonging to the same family.

earthwork A large mound, ditch, bank, or circle made of earth.

eclipse The disappearance of the sun or the moon in the shadow of another heavenly body.

empire A large area of land, including several different nations or peoples, governed by a single ruler called an emperor.

environment Humans' or animals' suroundings. Often used to describe landscape, climate, plants, and wildlife.

foundation The underground base that supports a building.

founded Started, set up (of a city).

frieze A band of decoration around a wall.

governor Ruler of part of an empire or kingdom, usually appointed.

guardian Someone who looks after weaker people.

Hercules An ancient Greek hero, famous for his bravery and strength.

hermit A person who lives alone and devotes much time to religion or philosophy.

Hindu A person who follows the Hindu religion, which grew up in India between around 1500-600 B.C. Hindus worship many gods, but they are all forms of Brahma, the supreme god.

incense A sweet-smelling substance, often used in religious ceremonies to clean the air and create a holy mood.

inherit To be given property when a relative dies.

irrigation Bringing water into dry land along specially built channels so that crops can grow there.

ivory The hard substance that elephant tusks are made of.

merchant A person who buys and sells goods.

Middle East The area located in southwestern Asia and northeastern Africa.

missionary A person who goes to another country to teach his or her religion.

mold A specially shaped piece of clay or stone into which liquid metal or wax is poured and allowed to set. Jewelry, tools, weapons, and statues were often made in molds.

monastery A place where people go to spend their lives praying and studying religion.

mosaic A picture made of little pieces of colored glass or stone carefully fitted together.

mummy A body that has been specially preserved before burial.

mutiny A rebellion by soldiers or sailors against their officers.

nomads People who have no settled home and who move from place to place in search of food for themselves or grazing land.

oracle A holy place where spirits lived. Priests and priestesses believed they could see into the future by understanding messages sent to them by the spirits.

papyrus An early form of paper, made from reeds.

philosophy A love of knowledge or wisdom; the search for truth.

pike A long pole with a sharp point and a cutting blade at the tip.

prow The front end of a ship.

rebellion A revolt against a ruler or government.

republic A country ruled by an elected leader, not by a king or queen.

reservoir A large pool or tank built to store water.

ritual Traditional way of observing a special, often religious, event.

sacrifice An offering made to please the gods.

sap The fluid that flows through veins in plants, carrying water and nourishment.

scholar Someone who spends his or her time studying.

scribe A specially trained person who kept written records of things, or who copied books by hand.

symbol Something that represents, or stands for, something else.

taxes Payments made to a ruler to support the government.

technology The science of developing tools and techniques to meet practical needs.

terra cotta Clay that has been baked in a special oven, called a kiln, at a fairly low temperature. It is usually a brick-red color.

tribe A group of people of the same race and culture.

tribute Valuable goods paid to rulers by people they have conquered.

wadi A watercourse that is dry except in the rainy season.

ziggurat A pyramid-shaped temple, with stepped sides.

INDEX

Aborigines 29, 41, 45, 46
Adena people 17, 35, 41, 46
Africa 16, 22-3, 27-8, 34, 40, 44
Ahura Mazda 42, 43
Alexander the Great 4-7, 16, 36, 43
Alexandria 16, 34
Americas 17, 23, 28-9, 35, 40-1, 45
Andes Mountain people 28, 29
Appius Claudius 19
Aristotle 30
Asoka of India 20, 38
astronomy 32
Athens 18, 37
Australasia 17, 23, 29, 35, 41, 45

Babylonians 32, 37
  beliefs 43
Buddhist religion 20, 38, 43, 46
burial mounds 17, 35, 41

calendars 35
Carthage 16, 27
Celtic people 13, 19, 25, 37, 43, 46
Chandragupta Maurya 15, 19, 38
Cheng, Prince of Qin 14, 21, 33, 39
Chifumbaze people 40, 46
China 14, 21, 27, 33, 39, 44

cities 16, 25, 26, 34
city-states 12, 16, 17, 18, 37, 46
cloth 28, 29, 40
Confucius 44
craft work 15, 16, 25, 34, 36-41

Daoism 44
Darius I and III 20, 21
democracy 18, 46
discoveries 30-5
Dreamtime 45

East Asia 14-15, 21-2, 27, 33, 39, 44
Egypt 16, 23, 28, 34, 44
elephants, war 22, 32
Etruscans 13, 46
Europe 12-13, 18-19, 25, 31, 36-7, 42-3
explorers 23, 31

farming 16, 17, 26, 27, 28
  in Europe 13, 24, 25
fishing 25, 26

gathering 15, 17, 25, 28, 29
glyphs 17, 35
gods and goddesses 22, 41, 42-5
gold working 34, 40
Great Serpent Mound 41
Great Wall of China 21, 33
Greeks 4, 5, 12, 18, 24, 31, 36
  beliefs 42, 43

Hannibal 22

herding 28
Hopewell people 17, 35, 41, 46
horoscopes 32
houses 25, 26, 28
hunting 13, 15, 17, 25, 28, 29

India 15, 19-20, 26, 32, 38, 43
Inuit people 29, 46
inventions 15, 30-5

jade 39
Japan 15, 22, 39
Jomon people 39, 46

Kush people 40

lacquer 39
leaders 18-23
lifestyles 24-9
lighthouse, Alexandria 34

Macedonians 4, 5, 7, 18
Maya people 17, 23, 35, 45, 46
medicine 31, 33
Meroë people 16, 28, 34, 40, 44
metalwork 13, 34, 40, 41
Middle East 13-14, 20, 26, 32, 37-8, 43, 47

Nabatean people 13, 46
Native Americans 17, 23, 29, 41, 45, 46
nature gods 43, 45
Nazca people 40, 46
Nok people 16, 34, 40
nomads 15, 17, 38, 47

Olmecs 17, 45, 46
Olympic Games 42

Pacific peoples 17, 35, 41, 45, 46

Paracas people 29, 40, 46
Parthenon 37
Pericles, General 18
Persepolis 20, 21, 37
Persian Empire 6, 14, 20, 26, 37
  beliefs 42, 43
Philip of Macedonia 5
Phoenicians 13, 16, 27, 46
pottery 16, 39, 40, 41
Ptolemy I 23, 34

Qin kingdom 14, 21, 27, 39

religious beliefs 42-5
rock paintings 29, 41
Romans 13, 16, 19, 22, 25, 31

satraps and satrapies 14, 20
schools, Indian 32
scientific discovery 30-5
Scythians 38, 46
shamans 45
Shang, Lord 27
Siberia 15
South Asia 15, 19-20, 26, 32, 38, 43
spirit beliefs 41, 44, 45
sun gods 45

terra-cotta soldiers 14, 39
time measurement 32
trade 16, 17, 25, 27
  Middle East 13, 26, 38

Warring States era 14
writing 17, 35

Yahweh 43
Yayoi people 15, 22, 39, 46

Zapotec people 17, 35, 46
Zoroaster 43